KW-327-660

NEGOTIATING

BULLET GUIDE

Karen Mannering

Hodder Education, 338 Euston Road, London NW1 3BH

Hodder Education is an Hachette UK company

First published in UK 2011 by Hodder Education

This edition published 2011

Copyright © 2011 Karen Mannering

The moral rights of the author have been asserted

Database right Hodder Education (makers)

Artworks (internal and cover): Peter Lubach
Cover concept design: Two Associates

All rights reserved. No part of this publication may be reproduced, stored in a retrieval system or transmitted in any form or by any means, electronic, mechanical, photocopying, recording or otherwise, without the prior permission in writing of Hodder Education, or as expressly permitted by law, or under terms agreed with the appropriate reprographic rights organization. Enquiries concerning reproduction outside the scope of the above should be sent to the Rights Department, Hodder Education, at the address above.

You must not circulate this book in any other binding or cover and you must impose this same condition on any acquirer.

British Library Cataloguing in Publication Data: a catalogue record for this title is available from the British Library.

10 9 8 7 6 5 4 3 2 1

The publisher has used its best endeavours to ensure that any website addresses referred to in this book are correct and active at the time of going to press. However, the publisher and the author have no responsibility for the websites and can make no guarantee that a site will remain live or that the content will remain relevant, decent or appropriate.

The publisher has made every effort to mark as such all words which it believes to be trademarks. The publisher should also like to make it clear that the presence of a word in the book, whether marked or unmarked, in no way affects its legal status as a trademark.

Every reasonable effort has been made by the publisher to trace the copyright holders of material in this book. Any errors or omissions should be notified in writing to the publisher, who will endeavour to rectify the situation for any reprints and future editions.

Hachette UK's policy is to use papers that are natural, renewable and recyclable products and made from wood grown in sustainable forests. The logging and manufacturing processes are expected to conform to the environmental regulations of the country of origin.

www.hoddereducation.co.uk

Typeset by Stephen Rowling/Springworks

Printed in Spain

Contents

Acknowledgements

I would like to acknowledge Adrian Greenwood and Richard Hemmings for their experience and help in forming my ideas for this book. I would also like to thank Alison Frecknall and Victoria Roddam.

About the author

Karen Mannering lives in Kent and is a specialist in people development with over 20 years' experience. Karen has a degree in Psychology and a Masters degree in management studies in addition to many skills-specific qualifications. She is a Fellow of the Institute of Personnel Development and a member of the British Psychological Society, the Chartered Management Institute and the Society of Women Writers and Journalists.

Karen's enthusiasm for lifelong learning and people development, together with her background in management, result in a practical but humanistic approach to introducing training into the workplace. Karen also contributes regularly to several magazines and has written many books on aspects of self-development. Her website can be found at www.karenmannering.co.uk.

Introduction

We often think of negotiating as a management skill, but in fact we all negotiate our way through the day in different situations, both at work and at home. Whatever the size of the deal you need to achieve – which might be anything from wanting to pull in a big order for the boss to persuading someone else in your household to do the washing up – you are still using negotiating tools and tactics.

Of course, getting the result you want is only one aspect of negotiating. We also need to consider the longer-term effects on the relationship. For example, will you need to meet (or work with) these people again? This is hugely important when considering what type of negotiating stance to take.

This book will take you swiftly through the entire negotiating minefield, so that whether you want to seal a work deal, or buy a house or a car, you can feel assured that you have achieved the best possible deal.

1 Negotiating: understanding the basics

Deal or no deal?

Have you ever felt the victim of a dodgy deal and vowed never to be in the same room as a sales professional again? Unfortunately you cannot avoid such situations; negotiations are a feature of daily life.

Whether you want to strike the deal of a lifetime in business or buy a used car, effective **negotiation** skills can help you get ahead of the game and move swiftly to a productive **settlement**.

Negotiations are a feature of daily life, so it pays to have effective negotiation skills
....

> **'Let us never negotiate out of fear.
> But let us never fear to negotiate.'**
> John F. Kennedy

Being able to negotiate with confidence will:

* increase your career prospects
* create openings for you in management
* allow you to make superb business contacts

and, let's not forget ....

* enable you to secure the best deal!

This chapter introduces the basic aspects of negotiating, and what to consider before you start.

What is negotiation?

The *Concise Oxford Dictionary* defines negotiation as:

Négōti|āte -1. confer (*with* another) with view to compromise or agreement. **2.** Arrange (affair), bring about (desired result), by negotiating.

Negotiation is:

* a process of exploring areas for agreement
* an opportunity to reach mutual understanding
* undertaken with positive intent
* an adult discussion that respects each party's views.

Negotiation is not:

* the recognition that disagreement is the starting point
* an opportunity to impose your will on the other party
* undertaken with a polarized view of a negative outcome
* war!

Negotiation is therefore a process to reach an agreement, whereby each party feels that they have had full input, been heard, and had their views considered. Mutual respect is helpful but not always vital to the outcome.

However, if one party does not trust the other party, this could have a significant negative effect. It may lead to the negotiation breaking down and not reaching a satisfactory outcome.

Negotiation is a process to reach an agreement

Size matters

Although negotiations may vary in complexity, there is a distinct difference between large-scale negotiations and smaller-scaled ones.

Large-scale negotiations	Small-scale negotiations
A minute taker on each side may be required	Own notes may be taken
May need a large room	Small space required
Often seated boardroom style	Informal seating
May include several parties	Usually between two parties

The size of your negotiation will dictate how you set up your room and how you behave. Larger-scale negotiations may need more preparation to ensure they run effectively, whereas smaller negotiations may be impromptu.

It's important that everyone who is key to agreeing an outcome must be present

Formal or informal?

The tone of your negotiation will decide whether it is formal or informal, and this will reflect on how people feel and behave when they attend the negotiation.

Formal	Informal
Agenda is produced before meeting	Often no agenda
Parties are invited to attend	Could be *ad hoc*
Meeting is recorded or **minute** taker is present	Both parties may take their own notes
Negotiation may have formal roles such as Chair and/or timekeeper	No set roles, everyone contributes

Setting expectations

Creating the right tone is also about setting up **expectations**. To make sure your negotiation stands a better chance of success, it is important that each party knows what to expect. You can convey this through your preparations.

To do this successfully, you will need to consider:

* the tone you feel is appropriate – formal or informal
* how you will invite all parties to the table
* how you will open the negotiation (often called the **'opening statement'**)
* whether either of you needs legal representation (as this could result in a change of tone)
* how the tone of the negotiation is conveyed by your environment and process.

Choosing the right time

If we feel nervous about a negotiation, we tend to rush in and immediately get down to the task. However, this may not be the most effective time for either party. For example, trying to negotiate with someone half an hour before they are due to leave the office will either result in them not making a decision or feeling bullied into one.

Neither of these outcomes is acceptable, as they will become breeding grounds for **resentment** and hostility. Choose the most appropriate time for both parties, and you will both come to the negotiating 'table' in a more positive frame of mind.

Consider:

* time of day
* time of week
* effects on attention, e.g. other events or looming tasks.

Creating the right atmosphere

The tone or subject of your negotiation may decide the **atmosphere**, but you also need to consider:

* the **venue** or room
* refreshments (for during the meeting and in breaks)
* whether you will need documents, paper, reports or evidence
* technical issues (will you need a laptop, telephone, presentation equipment?)
* how you will seat your guests and arrange the room
* interruptions and how you will handle them.

Case study

Phil wants to negotiate with Carol on a staff matter. Carol's manager, Sarah, will be going on maternity leave, and he would like to redistribute Sarah's work while Sarah is away. They are going to have to share this work because they cannot afford to employ an **interim** manager for a year.

Phil decides to hold this meeting in his office and to keep it as informal as possible. He invites Carol, giving her plenty of notice and telling her the subject of the meeting.

Phil wants Carol to feel comfortable and prepared for the discussion. This way, she enters the negotiation fully informed and ready to make a decision.

2 Negotiating and influencing

Where negotiating and influencing meet

Are you negotiating or are you **influencing**? When you are negotiating there is an even share of power. Each party has something the other party wants. However, influencing suggests a shift of power that feels unequal and possibly underhand.

Unfortunately it is only too easy to slip into this tricky area, especially when we turn to coaxing, cajoling or suggesting an outcome in our efforts to **persuade** the other person to give us a **preferential** deal.

Influencing suggests a shift of power that feels unequal
. . . .

> '**There is no such thing as a good influence.
> Because to influence a person
> is to give him one's own soul.**'
>
> Oscar Wilde

When we want a certain outcome in a deal, it is tempting to try to influence the outcome, but there is a big difference between a soft and a hard influence.

- ✔ *A soft influence is complimentary.*
- ✘ *A hard influence is coercive.*
- ✔ *A soft influence aids a fair negotiation.*
- ✘ *A hard influence is focused only on winning.*

Influence and attitude

We can exert a soft influence in a number of different ways, sometimes without even realizing it. It may be that we appear well groomed and professional, relaxed and friendly, confident in our facts, or what we say, and the other party reacts favourably to this.

Think about when you last saw a product on the TV and thought 'I'd like to buy one of those.' What was influencing you, the product itself or the image of the person and their lifestyle?

Even in a workplace negotiation, our **attitude** to the other person will have an impact on the level of influence they exert over the proceedings.

Be sure that any influence you exert is positive

If you and your negotiation partner intend to work together in the future, you need to be sure that any influence you exert is positive and helpful – not forced or underhand.

A word on influential inducements

These may be acceptable in a personal negotiation (for example offering to pay the legal fees on a new house to trigger the sale), but are highly unacceptable when they are a **bribe** (for example, 'I will pay you £10,000 to allow us to build a supermarket here').

> **Top tip**
> Don't give anything away without getting something in return, but *do* show the other party how their needs will be met.

Using your influence

It's important to understand just what positive influence means.

Positive influence is:

* welcomed and considered helpful by the other party
* within your personal style and delivery
* focused on the common outcome
* helpful, and accepted easily by the other party.

Positive influence is not:

* coercing or forcing someone to agree
* offering **inducements**, bribes or threats
* focused totally on self-interest
* feeling uncomfortable and 'squeezed' into a decision.

If you are still unsure, ask yourself:

Do I want to play an active part in reaching a positive deal that sits comfortably with us both, or do I just want to win at any cost?

Influencing skills

To some extent we all influence each other in life. However, those who exert soft and helpful influence on others demonstrate:

* a fair and balanced approach to the outcome
* an open and honest introduction to the issues
* the ability to take a back seat and let others go first.

Therefore the following skills are key:

1 **listening** – so that they clearly hear what the other party wants and needs
2 **questioning** - to probe for clarification
3 developing a **multiple viewpoint** – to see everyone's point of view.

Top tip
To improve rapport during a negotiation, aim to 'understand others first then be understood'.

How influential are you naturally?

☐ Do others tend to agree with you?
☐ Do you feel that you have good communication skills?
☐ Do you carefully consider the outcome of the negotiation first?
☐ Do you carefully consider what any other parties might want?
☐ Do you consider ways in which you both might benefit?
☐ Do you enjoy problem solving?
☐ Are you patient and understanding?

Don't worry if you did not tick all of these – they are all skills that can be developed.

Influencing skills can be developed

20

Could you be influential without realizing it?

Personal influence – some people are just very confident and personable as individuals. We sometimes describe them as having 'leadership qualities'. Other people naturally want to emulate them, and so they find themselves with a number of 'followers'.

If this is the case for you, you need to be very self-aware, so that you do not inadvertently influence where it is not appropriate.

Other forms of influence

Other forms of influence may be:

* **the ability to reward** – some people are put in a position where they can reward staff by providing resources, money, and allocating favourable projects. 'Vote for me and I will give you…'
* **the influential position** – where someone is in a position of note. 'You do know who I am?'
* **influential information** – information is power, and many people use it. 'If only you knew what I know!'
* **influential skills** – certain people have key skills that you may want or need. 'They need me…'
* **influentially connected** – where some people are only influential because of whom they know. 'Stick with me, kid, and I'll get you an introduction…'

None of these are necessarily negative – it is how you use or promote this influence that is important.

22

Case study

Phil recognizes that it would be easy to overly influence Carol. He has a rather dominant personality, and is aware that he could easily coerce Carol into taking on more of the work. He realizes that this could be counter-productive, because in the long run Carol could become resentful.

Phil understands that this would not make the basis of a good working relationship for the future. He suggests that they look at the work together and make joint decisions, splitting the work fairly.

3 Negotiating for win-win

Working towards win-win

When we go into a negotiation we not only need to consider the outcome but also the **quality** of the outcome.

If we are to negotiate a good deal for both sides, the outcome has to be robust enough to be workable for some time to come. In other words it has to have the ability to endure, and possibly be the underlying structure for other decisions.

> **The outcome of a negotiation has to be robust enough to be workable for some time to come**

> **'The law of win-win says,**
> **Let's not do it your way or my way;**
> **let's do it the best way.'**
> Greg Anderson

You cannot always guarantee the **outcome** of a negotiation, but you can:

* ensure that the process is **robust** and **fair**
* create a climate of open discussion
* work with your partner(s) to find a deal that suits you both
* build a solid negotiating relationship for the future.

The four perceptual positions

The result of any negotiation will be one of four perceptual positions:

1 win-lose (I win, you lose)
2 lose-win (I lose, you win)
3 lose-lose (we both lose)
4 win-win (we both win).

We will look at each one in turn to see what it offers both parties, how the outcome in each instance will change the relationship, and lay down the basis for any future negotiations.

Win-lose

In this position I win the negotiation and you lose. At the time it might seem a good outcome for me, but I am winning at your expense. If I never have to see you again, perhaps that is acceptable. I walk away richer and feeling more powerful. You are left sucking lemons.

But what if I had to work with you in the future? It is likely that you would:

* never **trust** me again
* view me as a bully
* think I was only interested in pursuing my own goal.

Is that a good basic framework for a future relationship?

Achieving success at the expense of others reflects a mindset based on a 'shortage' mentality, which suggests that there is not enough to go round for everyone.

Lose-win

In this position I lose the negotiation and you win. This is great for you as you now feel on top of the world, but it is not long until I start feeling resentful. Whether I blame you for winning or myself for being weak and ill prepared, I do not feel I want to meet with you again. I may even feel that the power ratio between us has shifted in your favour.

All in all, this is not a helpful way to continue in business, and it's a situation I would rather forget than be reminded of. Therefore I will not be seeking you out in the future. Even though you may think you have won you have lost, by damaging our relationship beyond repair.

Lose-win is not helpful in business

Lose-lose

Oh dear, what happened here? In this position we both lost. Perhaps neither of us negotiated a good deal, or we failed to reach a settlement – leaving us both feeling frustrated and dissatisfied.

On a positive note, if we recognize the situation in time, we could **adjourn** or rethink our approach, possibly setting another date in the near future to come together again.

Win-win

This is what we should be aiming for, both parties gaining from the negotiation. The outcome may not necessarily benefit both equitably, but there are **positive outcomes for each party**. For example:

I win

* I pay a lower price.
* I will give up my share on this project.
* I get to save six months of living costs and the opportunity to learn another language.

They win

* They have their money in advance.
* They offer me a share in another project.
* They want me to live abroad to undertake this role for six months.

The great thing about getting to win-win is that it preserves the relationship. You'll have no problems negotiating with this person again, and that builds a solid foundation for your future working relationship.

32

Win-win offers positive outcomes for each party

Getting to win-win

When you both work towards win-win, you will not only be negotiating fairly but you will also be sending the message to the other party that:

* you **value** their interaction
* you **care** about ensuring the outcome carries something for both of you
* you are entering the negotiation with **positive** intent
* you **believe** in the future of the relationship.

It therefore demonstrates more investment in the relationship than just ensuring you both walk away feeling satisfied. You show that you see your opponent as an ally, not an enemy.

Remember
In a negotiation, if you are ethical and honest it may cost you something, but you gain respect and trust.

Planning the way

To plan your way towards win-win, start by making a list of the **benefits** for both of you.

Ask yourself:

1 What would I like to gain from this negotiation?
2 What do I think they would like to gain from the negotiation?
3 Are there any hidden (or additional) benefits for me to gain?
4 Are there any hidden (or additional) benefits for them to gain?
5 Overall, what can we both gain from this joint negotiation?
6 Outside this negotiation, are there other areas of business or opportunities where we could work together?

This exercise will help you cultivate a positive attitude towards the negotiation, which will make success much more likely. It will also improve the relationship between the two sides.

Case study

Phil knows that Carol has more experience in some areas of Sarah's work than he does. In these instances she would be the most appropriate person to undertake them. However, he also knows that they would both like to cover some of Sarah's other projects because they are high profile and would develop them as professionals.

Phil makes a list of these and also tries to anticipate which ones Carol will go for. At this stage he is clear that there must be a win-win outcome for them both, and he is keen to work towards that.

4 Understanding strategy and tactics

Researching your options

As part of selecting your perceptual position (as detailed in the previous chapter), you'll need to be clear what your options are at both a **strategic** and **tactical** level. You will then be able to engage fully in the meeting and reduce the amount of 'thinking on your feet' required, as this is when mistakes can be made.

By researching your options in advance, you'll reduce the risk of regretting a decision made hastily during the meeting, which you then have to live with.

> **By researching your options in advance, you'll reduce the risk of regretting a hasty decision**

> **'Strategy without tactics is the slowest route to victory. Tactics without strategy is the noise before defeat.'**
>
> Sun Tzu

Know the difference between your strategic and tactical options:

* Strategic options are your end game.
* Strategic options set the long-term future.
* Tactical options are your offers and **concessions**.
* Tactical options are your bargaining power.

Wants, needs and concessions

To begin your preparation it's helpful to be honest about your own wants and needs. Why is the negotiation taking place? What would you (ideally) like the outcome to be?

Break your overall outcome down into each point that needs negotiation. Divide it into a table like this one:

Wants	Would like	Concession? Yes or no
The project to install the new computer system	A role in the project to install a new computer system	No – I need a part in this
To attend the conference in May	To attend some professional conference this year	Yes
To lead the project on 'Better Communication'	To be an active part of the 'Better Communication' project	Yes

Concessions are points that you are either happy to give up or that you are able to use for further negotiation.

As you saw on the previous page, the person concerned would be prepared to give up two of their 'wants' and 'would likes' if pressed, but they would not wish to give up the installation of the new computer project, even if they only had a contributory role on that project.

Concessions are bargaining tools to use for further negotiation

Ranking your concessions

It is imperative that these concessions are not just given up but 'cashed in' to enable you to gain most of the outcomes that you really want.

To help with this it is useful to rank your concessions, so that in a negotiation you know instantly which concessions you should be offering up first. An example is shown below. (Ten is something you will resist losing, and one is something you would easily concede.)

Wants	Would like	Concession? Yes or no	Rank
The project to install the new computer system	A role in the project to install a new computer system	No – I need a part in this	10
To attend the conference in May	To attend one professional conference this year	Yes	2
To lead the project on 'Better Communication'	To be an active part of the 'Better Communication' project	Yes	8

Now you need to **imagine that you are the other party** undertaking the same activity. Naturally you cannot anticipate exactly their wants and needs, but you can make an educated guess.

Ask yourself:

- ✳ What do I think the benefits are for them?
- ✳ Where do I think they may be likely to make concessions?
- ✳ What will be the most important projects, items or issues that they will want to manage/own/solve?
- ✳ What means most to them?
- ✳ How do you think they would rank their choices?

What are the benefits for the other party?

Completing your matrix

Using your ranking system and also the information you gleaned
from the previous exercise, start to pull together a table of possible
concessions. From this you can estimate the probability of an agreement,
as shown below.

Point	Rank	Possible negotiation	Probability of acceptance
The project to install the new computer system	No concession 10	No	–
To attend the conference in May	2	To run a new policy workshop	70%
To lead the project on 'Better Communication'	8	To sit on the 'Better Communication' board as department lead	50%

Thinking outside the box #1

An ordered approach, taken in your own time, means that during the meeting you'll not need to make snap decisions. With your **matrix** by your notes you'll immediately know whether you would be willing to agree to a request. However, we also need to think 'outside the box'.

This is your opportunity to be radical. You may have other concessions or opportunities you can offer that are outside this negotiation. For example, you may not be able to negotiate on price, but can you include other things not strictly in line with the negotiation, such as:

* a donation to charity?
* a work placement for a school leaver?
* the possibility of a negotiation on another project?

'Start out with an ideal and end up with a deal.'
Karl Albrecht

Thinking outside the box #2

Another way of thinking outside the box is to consider the possibility of dividing or joint work. For example, you may not be able to **concede** on a project but you may be able to work together on it, sharing the task.

Top tip
This particular win-win approach may even forge bonds for other future joint work projects, as it will reveal just how well you work together.

Case study

Phil writes down all the parts of Sarah's work that he knows about. He realizes that other projects might come up during her time off, but he cannot **anticipate** those. He puts the projects into a ranking order for himself and then does the same activity again, ranking the ones he thinks Carol will go for.

When he compares the lists he realizes that there may be some areas that she will not want anyway, and some he is less worried about losing. He is also considering discussing some joint working on the high-profile projects, so that they both benefit from the exposure.

5 Building rapport

The importance of building rapport

Building **rapport** is key to performing as an excellent negotiator. When we build rapport with others, we are putting in place the essential building blocks for all future **communication**. We will then be able to communicate with others on their wavelength, making messages so much easier to transmit and be understood.

Building rapport is more than copying body language; it holds the key to the way we interact with others.

Building rapport holds the key to the way we interact with others
....

> **'Negotiation talks are the best way to solve anything. We must replace wars and weapons with negotiations and talks.'**
>
> Akbar Ganji

Building rapport is also a necessary skill for building **trust**.

Trust is a small word with big implications.

* By working towards win-win we naturally start to build trust.
* Both parties need to work towards building trust *in addition* to other business outcomes.
* If trust is broken by either party, it can become pointless to continue with the negotiation.

The animal within

We are all essentially animals. That's why we react to one another's body language and feelings at a much deeper level than we may consciously understand. If you've ever thought, 'I know that person is unwell,' or had a 'gut feeling' about someone, that's your **animal instinct** at work, picking up hidden signals.

You might even call it **intuition**, but we all give out signals and react to the signals we receive back. These signals can work with us to create deeper bonds, or against us to make us feel we have nothing in common with a person, perhaps even to the extent of being repelled by them.

Awareness of this animal instinct, or intuition, is a vital tool to use when we are trying to build rapport.

52

What are we doing when we build rapport?

When we try to build rapport with someone we:

* use techniques to try and speed up the relationship
* use high-calibre communication methods to relay messages
* help the other person receive any message in an acceptable way.

We are not:

* trying to manipulate the outcome
* bullying
* trying to teach them anything
* being patronizing!

53

Rapport building through body language

Have you ever noticed that when two people know each other well, they automatically mirror each other's body language? They walk the same way, and hold their bodies in similar positions. In essence, they are automatically in rapport with each other. They find **comfort** and bond through being similar.

Where possible (and being unobtrusive), try to match your partner's body language. Also try:

* sitting slightly forward to show keenness
* using similar arm motions to describe situations
* holding and moving your head in the same way as your negotiating partner
* positioning your whole body in a similar way.

Eye contact and rapport

When considering eye contact:

Do

✔ maintain steady eye contact
✔ look down and refer to
   your notes
✔ be conscious of habits, e.g.
   gazing into the distance
   while speaking
✔ choose which emotions to show

Don't

✘ stare
✘ be afraid of looking anywhere
   other than at the other person
✘ be too expressive with your
   eyes; it can be viewed as
   unprofessional
✘ give the game away with
   your eyes

Remember

Good eye contact does not mean a continual gaze,
but rather the avoidance of shifty eyes, especially
when the other person is speaking to you.

Rapport building through verbal signals

Watching what you say is not only about the words. We constantly give verbal signals, from the 'OK' to show we are listening and understanding through to the gentle 'Mmmm' to demonstrate that we are considering that point.

Try this!

To realize just how important this rapport-building signal is, ask a colleague to stay silent while you try to speak to them – it feels unnatural and uncomfortable.

Top tip
To create and maintain rapport it is essential to provide these **subtle signals**, and be aware of the messages we are giving.

Rapport building through breathing techniques

You may never have taken much notice of your breath, but our breathing is the most subtle of all rapport-building techniques. When we are in rapport, we breathe at the same depth and pace as our colleagues, and our bodies feel comfortable and safe. By matching our breathing to another person's, we demonstrate **empathy** without being aware of it.

Try this!

The next time someone comes up to you, panting because they are late, instead of telling them to calm down, surreptitiously match their breathing and then slowly return to normal breathing, while talking to them. You'll notice that they will take their breathing pace down with you.

Our breathing is the most subtle of all rapport-building techniques

Pacing and leading

The exercise on the previous page is a type of rapport building called pacing and leading. Essentially you are using a technique that takes the other person along with you by creating rapport. You can do this by using:

* body language
* eye contact
* verbal signals
* breathing.

Pacing and leading should allow your negotiating partner to be far more **open** to your communication, and **receptive** to your ideas.

Case study

In addition to the preparation that Phil has done around his own wants and concessions, he also spends time considering Carol. He's aware that he can appear over-confident and assertive, and doesn't want this to influence the negotiation. He wants Carol to feel comfortable with the outcome, not steamrollered.

Phil has noticed that Carol does not react well to his direct approach and focused looks. He therefore reconsiders his use of eye contact, aiming to create a more encouraging and inclusive relationship. He is also aware that he taps the table when he wants the conversation to move faster – but recognizes that this tends to irritate the other person.

6 Analysing positions and setting your strategy

The overall strategy

It is now time to consider your overall strategy for the negotiation. You'll need to think about your tactics, and whether you need to have certain people in key positions.

This section describes planning *how* the negotiation will take place. You may be tempted to leave out this part of the planning in your keenness to get started, but that would be a big mistake.

How you organize your negotiation can play as large a part in its success as the content
....

'The most difficult thing in any negotiation, almost, is making sure that you strip it of the emotion and deal with the facts.'

Howard Baker

To move the negotiation along, you now need to consider:

* whether you need to have people playing **key roles**
* an **overall strategy** for the negotiation
* a range of tactical **manoeuvres**
* how you will take forward your bidding.

Roles and the games people play

Whatever role people take, their function is ultimately to move the negotiation forward in different ways. (Some of them may be underhand – so watch out for them.)

1 The Chair or **Facilitator** keeps everyone on track.
2 The **Minute Taker** records the discussions and decisions.
3 The **Timekeeper** ensures it does not overrun.
4 The **Critic** questions judgements and picks holes in every outcome.
5 The **Good Guy** pours soothing oil on troubled waters and brings the negotiators back together again.

Problems arise when you either do not recognize the roles being played or do not have any yourself. This will leave you open to the opposition playing games with you such as the Critic wading in and then the Good Guy appearing to be your best friend.

Setting the strategy

An overall strategy sets the focus for the negotiation and provides a goal for both parties to work towards. For this reason it's crucial that the strategy is **shared** and **clarified** with everyone attending the negotiation. You can do this at the beginning of the meeting or even beforehand.

The strategy could form the title of the agenda. With everyone present then clear about the desired outcome, the negotiation can stay focused and time wasting is kept to a minimum.

Tactics

After the strategy is set, you will have to take a number of tactical measures. These define the **approach** you are going to follow. A huge range of tactics could be employed, and therefore we cannot detail them all. However, the following four tactics are the most popular:

* bidding high
* bidding low
* bidding first
* bidding last.

Each of these will be discussed on the next four pages.

Your tactics will define the approach you are going to follow during the negotiation

Four tactics in action

Bidding high

You may wonder why you would do this. In bidding high you go in with a high offer – with a **condition**. For example, 'I will pay the full price but I want to sign the contracts today.' Essentially, you are trying to cut out all other possible bidders. It can be fast and almost non-negotiation, but it can also mean that you both get what you want.

Benefits of bidding high	Disadvantages of bidding high
You are very likely to secure the deal	You may have paid over the odds
You can get what you want fast and can move on to the next stage – everything is sorted	You have not tested the price in the marketplace
If you find negotiating uncomfortable, you can skip the process	You risk looking desperate and the price rising further

Bidding low

Some people always believe in starting low, especially if they are not certain of the price the other person is looking for. However, you can irritate the other party if they suspect you of not being professional or serious in your approach.

In some cultures, it is expected that any negotiation will start from positions that are far apart and that you will meet somewhere in the middle; in other cultures this is not the case.

Benefits of bidding low	Disadvantages of bidding low
You might get a great deal	The other party may think you are not serious and lose patience with you
You can always raise your bid, but it's difficult to negotiate down if you go in too high	You risk looking like a cheap organization, and that may raise concerns
You can offer other options (for example low money but service extras)	You risk being trumped by someone else offering more

Bidding first

When someone says 'Who wants to go first?' do you leap in or hang back? Like playing on home turf, some people believe there is an advantage in being the first to get your point across or set out your stall. Others may prefer to delay declaring their position until they see what everyone else is offering.

Benefits of bidding first	Disadvantages of bidding first
The first bid sets the tone	Everyone sees your bid first and may adapt their bids accordingly
You can set out your stall first (anyone following will seem as if they are copying your bid)	You may hear something later that you wished you had copied
You get the chance to make some great points that seem fresh on first hearing	You may have misunderstood the whole situation and it is too late to change track

Bidding last

You may decide that the best tactic is to go last. This has a number of issues attached to that decision. For example, it can easily seem like a done deal if the first bid was a strong one.

Benefits of bidding last	Disadvantages of bidding last
In complex negotiations you may acquire more information about the project as you progress	Your points can sound repetitive and you have nothing new to say
You can wait and then trump everyone else's deal	You can appear like an 'also ran' rather than a key contender
If the other bids were unacceptable, you will appear at the end like a 'white knight', ready to rescue the project	It can appear that you are hanging back and are not enthusiastic

Case study

Phil believes the strategy for his meeting with Carol is to apportion Sarah's work fairly for the period of her leave. He will start the negotiation by clarifying this with Carol so that they are both working towards the same goal.

Phil plans to ask Carol to say first which of Sarah's projects interest her. He is hoping that, by using this tactic, there will be a couple of projects that he can easily agree to. This will leave him in a strong position when he states that, as she has some quick wins, the others should be his.

Phil does not believe that anyone else needs to be involved, and therefore he will not need to adopt any forced positions.

7 Changing positions

Dealing with changing positions

'Shifting sands' can make negotiating both interesting and frustrating. Just when you feel ready to seal a deal, the other side may propose a change, and you have to react. This is where your preparation can really pay off.

Negotiations are subject to change. Part way through your negotiation either party may feel the need to:

* change their stance on some issue
* **reframe** their point of view
* ask for more
* change some **concessions**.

If you have prepared by creating a range of options, you won't be caught out

> **'Unless you are prepared to give up something valuable you will never be able to truly change at all, because you'll be forever in the control of things you can't give up.'**
>
> Andy Law

Some parties will introduce change at the last minute as an underhand tactic: for example, a person may raise the price of something the day before contracts are due to be signed, leaving the other party with little room for manoeuvre.

This chapter shows you how to understand the thinking behind changing positions, how to manage the risk and how to stay flexible.

Why change positions?

Negotiations are living, breathing processes. During a negotiation, new facts may come to light that require you to **reassess** the situation. For example, the fine details of how you would spend or invest £10,000 might change considerably if it was suddenly revealed that the sum was in fact £100,000.

Also, as you find out more about what the other party wants, you might change your own wants and needs. You only have to watch house buying programmes on TV to see that the needs the customer states at the beginning of the search may bear no relation to the type of house they actually buy!

Negotiations are living processes

About turn or gentle curve?

Not all changes of position form a dramatic U-turn. Some are gentle curves that can be accommodated within the negotiation. For example, one party may decide that their list of wants is actually slightly longer than before, or that they want to make fewer concessions.

If the change is a significant one, it might be better to return to the beginning of the negotiation and set out both parties' wants and needs in light of these changes – in other words, start again. If it is only a small change, try to maintain relations while **incorporating** these new needs into your general discussions.

WIIFT? WIIFM?

If either or both parties change their position on any aspect of the negotiation, you will have to think effectively on your feet. The quickest way to do this is to adjourn briefly and work out **WIIFT** and **WIIFM**.

What's In It For Them?

* They must have had a reason for changing their stance. What has changed since setting out the negotiation?
* Has it suddenly occurred to them that they would be better off doing it the new way?
* Where are the benefits?
* Should I be worried?

What's In It For Me?

* If I agree to the changes, what can I expect out of the deal?
* Will they concede on other items?
* How important is this new issue?
* What could it be worth?

If either party changes position, you'll have to work out WIIFT and WIIFM

Managing the risk

There is a risk to changing positions. The ultimate risk is that the negotiation falls flat and you are into lose-lose (as discussed in chapter 3). Other risks might be:

* One party now appears needy or greedy.
* **Suspicion** grows as each party speculates on why the other is changing.
* Both parties put greater value on certain projects.
* While negotiating over smaller details, the main eye is 'off the ball' and the **focus** can be lost.

All these potential risks can be managed if you **consider them in advance** and integrate any concerns into a negotiation agreement.

Staying flexible

Changing positions requires you to be flexible and think nimbly.

1 Keep all options open.
2 Resist being **pressurized** – ask for time out to consider.
3 Try to think of this as an **opportunity** (they might offer up another concession).
4 If so, ask for your largest 'want' in response.
5 Don't be afraid to ask them why they have changed position.
6 Don't be afraid to change position yourself.

Finally, do remember that you do not have to agree. Their request to change may make the negotiation null and void.

Keep all options open

Typical changes in position #1

Parties may change their position in many different ways. These are some of the most typical:

Changing the deal

* **Remember** – you don't have to go along with it if you perceive it as unfair.
* Ask for time out to reconsider and gain more background information.
* Take any future deal more slowly, check each detail and sign contracts (with preventative clauses included) as you go.

Wanting to pull out

* This could be an empty threat or a real one.
* It could be a possible attempt to force a decision either way.
* It can be an indication of tiredness or frustration – suggest a break or creative **intervention**.

Typical changes in position #2

Asking for more

* Consider whether this is possible.
* Reassess your value on the project.
* Don't be afraid to match this with your own wants.

Reducing timescales

* Check this against reality; you may not be able physically to do this.
* Assess this against costs; some people are willing to pay a lot more for a speedier completion.
* Do not agree to anything that could cause problems later.

Introducing another party

* Attempt to clarify how and why this party was not mentioned earlier.
* Point out that the new party, if they are to join the negotiation, may need to sign up to some form of **confidentiality agreement**.
* Consider beginning again now that the dynamics have changed.

Case study

Carol is thinking about the aspects of Sarah's job that she would like to take on. Phil has mentioned his wish to take on one particular project. At the time, Carol said, 'No worries', but she now thinks it makes more sense for her to take it forward. It plays to her strengths, and will also provide evidence for her training programme.

Carol is concerned that this will look like a turn-around to Phil, as he believes that particular project is now his. She decides to look again at her own list of projects and concessions, and to try to ensure that Phil takes this information in the right way so that it does not ruin their working relationship.

8 Handling objections

Considering objections

Objections are a fundamental part of negotiating. Expect at least one

Imagine the situation: you've worked on what you want, made intelligent guesses at what the other party wants, and thought about how these will combine to create a perfect outcome. Your preparation feels certain, and you couldn't possibly expect the other party to object to your ideas or any part of the deal.

But then they do. Whatever can you do? Suddenly you picture the negotiation crumbling in front of you.

First of all, you need thinking time, so refrain from acting rashly. Take the following steps:

* clarify the detail of the objection
* work out what this means to you and how it affects your stance
* call a short break to reconsider the facts
* return to the negotiation with a revised plan.

'Nothing will ever be attempted if all possible objections must first be overcome.'

Samuel Johnson

Reacting to objections

Objections are stronger than areas of disagreement. If the other party objects to some issue, you need to understand what lies behind the problem. Try the following.

1 Stop talking and start **listening**.
2 Use **probing questions** to clarify the main point of their objection.
3 Listen with your eyes as well as your ears (what are body language and facial expression telling you?).
4 Consider what is *not* being said.
5 Is it a surface issue or misunderstanding? Does it run deeper? Perhaps it is value or culture based?

In essence, you need to put yourself in the position of the other party – see things from their angle. Do they have a point?

When objections are raised, a gulf seems to open up between the two parties. Suddenly we appear very different, when earlier we seemed to be in accord.

We need to get back to building bridges. Here are some ways to do this.

✔ Do keep the communication going.
✔ Do return to the overall strategy.
✔ Do work forwards again, finding common ground and links.
✔ Do use positive language: 'How interesting' or 'Let's explore this further'.

✘ Don't go off in a fit of pique.
✘ Don't assume that this automatically ends the relationship.
✘ Don't decide that there are too many differences between you.
✘ Don't use negative or patronizing language such as 'Well, it is obvious that you...'

Strengthening your case

Depending on the subject and nature of the objection, there could be great advantage in retreating to strengthen your case. If it might improve the situation, consider incorporating ideas as shown in the diagram.

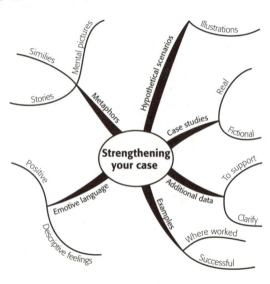

Using humour

Using **humour** can be either hugely therapeutic or a complete disaster, depending on the way it is used and perceived.

Humour used appropriately can:

* lighten the issue
* soften the objection
* raise the **morale** in the room.

Humour used inappropriately can:

* be viewed as **poor judgment**, insensitive, or crass
* cause **polarization** where the gulf between parties widens
* lower the morale in the room.

Top tip
If you are unsure about using humour – don't!

Paint some hypothetical scenarios

Sometimes the root of an objection is that the other party cannot **envisage** the new world you are portraying. For example, if you are negotiating for a new housing development to be built on a particular site, the other party may not be able to envisage it being there and object to that particular site being used.

In this situation our hypothetical scenarios would follow a typical day in the life of the A N Other family and try to depict how they would interact in our favoured environment. We would be attempting to remove objections by describing how our favoured site really is the most appropriate choice.

Be open to compromise

Constructing a compromise

Where objections run deep and it's clear that the other party is not going to move away from their position without some aspect of change, you will need to **change your tactics** towards constructing a **compromise**.

Compromise can bring the parties back together, as it demonstrates that:

* you are both still willing to negotiate
* you are open to ideas and options
* neither party is looking for an outright win on all their wants
* you can both work together
* you hope to continue the relationship into the future.

Third-party intervention

Introducing a third party, such as a **facilitator**, is not a sign of weakness or a cry for help. An expert facilitator can help put you both back on track and thinking in the same direction once again.

If there are deep-seated difficulties, a facilitator trained in **mediation** can help both parties to work through their differences, and the resulting relationship may be even stronger.

Introducing a third party is not a sign of weakness

94

Case study

Phil and Carol finally meet to discuss Sarah's work projects. However, Carol is finding Phil quite aggressive in his tactics and delivery. Although they mostly agree on which of them will take on which project, there is one that Phil has assumed is naturally his. Carol objects to this assumption, as she believed that everything was up for discussion.

Phil admits that perhaps he was assuming too much and that he would like to go back a step and start that part of the negotiation again. Although Carol is happy with this, it has made her slightly guarded with Phil, and he needs to work hard to regain her trust.

9 Staying in control

Managing your stress

Don't underestimate how stressful negotiations can be. Even the excitement of winning a deal does not instantly smooth away the hours of preparation and the **tension** of the meeting. It is not over yet, as nothing has been signed, and even waiting comes with its own pressures. Throughout this time you need to be able to manage your feelings.

You need to be able to manage your own feelings, as no one can do this for you

> **'Stress is an ignorant state. It believes that everything is an emergency.'**
>
> Natalie Goldberg

Learning to **recognize** your own body's reaction to stress, and being able to keep a clear head in a crisis, is a useful skill for many situations. During a negotiation, too much stress can cause:

* impaired thinking
* heightened emotions
* snap decisions
* deals you might regret.

The fight or flight response

Our bodies are designed to react in two ways to a stressful situation:

* fight it

* run away from it.

These are often called the **fight** and **flight reflexes**. You will release hormones that cause your heart to pump blood around your body faster and your breathing to become shallow and fast. However, if you are sitting in a room negotiating, you are unable to react to this surge of hormones, which will have a negative effect on your body.

This stress reaction could result in you:

* feeling sick
* having a headache
* experiencing a panic attack

or generally feeling (and looking) unwell.

'Know thyself'

Just as we might experience headaches differently, we don't all experience stress in the same way. The most common feeling described is one of tension, but where you feel it can vary. In the following list, tick the areas where you feel tension.

- ☐ Head area
- ☐ Jaw
- ☐ Neck
- ☐ Upper shoulder region

- ☐ Across the back
- ☐ Down your arms and/or legs
- ☐ In your fingers or toes
- ☐ Stomach area

Feeling the onset of tension can be a helpful warning signal, so don't ignore it. When you start to feel tense, recognize that something has to change.

When you start to feel tense, recognize that something has to change

Stressful situations

Some **situations** cause us to feel tense and stressed too. For example, if we are naturally tidy, being expected to work in an untidy work area will create tension. The more we get to know ourselves, the better we will be able to recognize tension forming. We can then put in place counter measures.

In this list, what situations make you feel tense?

☐ Being with someone you don't know
☐ Doing a presentation
☐ Not really understanding the material or the issue
☐ Being with very senior or important people
☐ Having to think on your feet
☐ Discussing figures knowledgeably
☐ Dealing with statistics

Any others? Write them here.

102

Improving the negotiating environment

We have established that:

* stress and tension are normal
* you don't need any additional factors to make them worse.

Therefore let's look at what makes the best negotiating **environment**.

* Select a room with a pale decor (bright colours can become unsettling).
* Choose a room that incorporates some calming elements (such as plants or a fish tank).
* Provide comfortable chairs and possibly a flat surface to put your papers on. Make sure that the room is neither too hot nor too cold, and has enough air circulating to keep your energy levels high.
* Ensure that you have some refreshments to hand; you may be there some while.

Loosen off muscles

In the meeting, you might need to **loosen** your muscles to keep tension at bay. Do this discreetly, as the other party could misconstrue your movements: stretching your arms to loosen the upper back may be interpreted as boredom.

* If you are sitting at a table that covers your legs, rotate your ankles or stretch your legs out.
* Sit upright, pull your shoulders down a little and then relax. Do the same by pulling your shoulders back.
* Clench and relax your buttocks and/or shift your position.

These stretching moves are hardly noticeable, but can make a big difference. If the other party leaves the room, take the opportunity to have a full body stretch.

Use breathing techniques

When we feel tension, our breathing becomes shallower and we do not allow sufficient **oxygen** into our lungs. This is not helped if we are in a sitting position, as it automatically shortens the torso.

At moments of tension:

1 take a deep breath in through the nose
2 hold for the count of three
3 exhale in a controlled manner (also for the count of three) through the mouth
4 repeat three times.

You may feel your body relax down as you exhale. Imagine the tension leaving your body as you breathe out, and try to picture yourself in one of your favourite places – perhaps on a beach or in a field.

Prevent stress build-up

Many people feel their stress levels rising when they are put in a position for which they are not ready. This is why it's so important to do as much **preparation** as possible. Feeling **organized** and in **control** will cut down on the amount of tension you experience.

Outside work, ensure you have both an absorbing hobby and a form of exercise. In addition, watch your diet. Your body is an engine that needs good, wholesome food to operate effectively. Feed your body the nutrients it deserves, and it will reward you with optimum functioning.

Case study

Phil and Carol are both feeling stressed about the negotiation. Phil is concerned that Carol seems tense, and that he is being more forceful than helpful. He decides to back off and call a break to the proceedings.

Carol is tense because she has put effort into securing a few key projects and fears she will lose them. She is pleased when Phil suggests a break and decides to go for a fast walk around the block.

She suggests that when they convene, they revisit the projects apportioned so far. Phil thinks that is a great idea, as his strategy is still to have a great working relationship with Carol, and he wants to reiterate that.

10 Closing the deal

The vital closing steps

At the end of a negotiation, when all the decisions have been put in place and an **outcome** has been verbally agreed, it is tempting to move swiftly on to celebration. But you could find that you are partying prematurely.

Health warning!

All the hard work you have just put in can easily unravel if you forget to undertake some vital closing steps. Ignore this final stage at your peril.

Ignore the vital closing steps at your peril

●●●

> **'If you can't go around it, over it, or through it, you had better negotiate with it.'**
> Ashleigh Brilliant

Closing the deal effectively is important because it:

* ties up any loose ends
* summarizes all the facts
* formalizes the relationship
* signals that the negotiation is complete.

There will be plenty of time to crack open the champagne *after* you have closed the deal effectively.

'Let's just summarize'

Regrettably, gone is the day when a handshake sealed a **deal**. Your negotiated outcome needs to be brought together professionally, and recorded.

* Close your negotiation with a **summary**, not just of the points gained by each party but also of the process.
* Detail any concessions, and congratulate the other party on the outcome.
* To do this effectively, use a flip chart or some form of presentation equipment that everyone can see. List each issue and the accompanying outcome, so that everyone is clear regarding both the journey and the destination.

Clarity + honesty + agreement = a great deal

Reciprocity

When we discussed win-win in chapter three, it was clear that each party should benefit from the deal if at all possible. This will help facilitate excellent working relations in the future. However, now is the moment to revisit this one more time, to make sure that everyone has benefited in some way from the negotiation.

It is not too late to identify that someone has not benefited sufficiently, and to offer something else. In addition, the **law of reciprocity** is that, one party having given something, the other party feels able (and in some cultures, duty bound) to reciprocate. Therefore you may benefit further from giving more away.

Last-minute disagreements

In the same way that there may be last-minute agreements, there may also be last-minute disagreements. Perhaps someone misheard something, or has since thought better of the deal.

Last-minute disagreements can be quite difficult as it can mean 'back to the drawing board'. You need to remember that the other party will not sign and seal a deal until they are **satisfied** with the outcome.

Top tip
Try to see disagreements as an opportunity to revisit items, rather than disasters – and stay positive.

Handling a package deal

When you present your final summary, try to encourage the other party to view the outcome as a **package** rather than items on which they win or lose. For example, each job we have is an employment package. In one job we may be paid more but have less holiday entitlement, in another there might be a greater pension incentive but less flexible hours.

Rationalizing in this way demonstrates that we generally don't get everything we want, but when viewed as a package we have an overall acceptable deal.

By packaging the deal up, you will lose the nuances of who won what, and allow the other party to congratulate themselves on securing what is probably, overall, a reasonable outcome for them (and for you too).

View the outcome as a package

Creating a contract

Contracts can be typed up immediately or sent through later.

Benefits of now	Benefits of later
You can get the magic signature now	Both parties can think about things
There is less chance of the other party reneging on any point	There is no waiting around after the deal
You can start implementing the plan immediately	You can inform other parties who may need to know, and whose agreement is required

Essentially, the contract needs to include the following:

1 the detailed subject of the negotiation
2 the **outcome**, including any details of who is now doing what task
3 **timescales** and deliverables
4 **quality** measures, monitoring, and future dates
5 signatures (with dates).

Building in revisiting dates

Quite often your outcomes will need **revisiting** from time to time. This may be to ensure that everything is on track, or it could be a complete 'back to the negotiating table' once again.

Even if **monitoring** is not part of the deal, it may be pertinent to incorporate some dates for revisiting the contract, as this can form an important part of the relationship. Meeting again periodically provides opportunities to:

* keep the relationship going
* discuss **expectations** and outcomes
* discuss any new projects or side shoots from the original project
* **re-allocate** if the **parameters** have changed.

Above all, revisiting outcomes on a regular basis will improve information flow and understanding between the parties.

What did you learn?

Negotiating a deal is a huge learning activity. You are learning about:

Increasingly, organizations and authorities are requiring us to maintain records of **continuous professional development (CPD)**. The negotiating table offers so many opportunities for this.

Record your experience and reflect on what you could have done differently, and you have an excellent basis for your future development.

Case study

Phil and Carol are happy with the results of their negotiation. Although it took time to prepare, organize and run, they are both sure that the outcome will take them through the time that Sarah is away.

They also identified that, during the process, they learnt a lot about each other. They hope this will enhance their working relationship. They established that they also had to create a process for allocating new work.

They each recorded, in a learning log, which skills they used and what they would do differently next time. Both agreed that they had developed their ability to negotiate – a skill they will use again in the future.

What next?

Throughout this book I have tried to give you some tools and techniques to help you negotiate in all situations. I hope I have covered most circumstances, but if you would like to read further on this subject, you might find these books and websites useful.

Gates, Steve, *The Negotiation Book: Your Definitive Guide to Successful Negotiating* (London: John Wiley & Sons, 2010)

Kennedy, Gavin, *Essential Negotiation* (New York: Bloomberg Press, 2009)

The Project Management Institute at http://www.pmi.org has many features regarding negotiation within the context of project management.

The Chartered Management Institute at http://www.managers.org.uk has a good range of articles and training courses covering negotiation skills.